CASHLYN WISDOM

Money and Finance Strategies For Kids

Empower Financial Responsiblity, Budgeting Skills, Saving Habits, Goal Setting In Preparation For Tomorrow

Copyright © 2024 by Cashlyn Wisdom

All rights reserved. No part of this publication may be reproduced, stored or transmitted in any form or by any means, electronic, mechanical, photocopying, recording, scanning, or otherwise without written permission from the publisher. It is illegal to copy this book, post it to a website, or distribute it by any other means without permission.

Cashlyn Wisdom asserts the moral right to be identified as the author of this work.

Cashlyn Wisdom has no responsibility for the persistence or accuracy of URLs for external or third-party Internet Websites referred to in this publication and does not guarantee that any content on such Websites is, or will remain, accurate or appropriate.

Designations used by companies to distinguish their products are often claimed as trademarks. All brand names and product names used in this book and on its cover are trade names, service marks, trademarks and registered trademarks of their respective owners. The publishers and the book are not associated with any product or vendor mentioned in this book. None of the companies referenced within the book have endorsed the book.

First edition

This book was professionally typeset on Reedsy. Find out more at reedsy.com

Contents

Introduction	1
Setting Financial Goals for Kids	4
Saving and investing for kids	13
Entrepreneurship Education for Kids	18
Make Learning Fun	21
Addressing Challenges and Pitfalls for Kids	25
Be Patient and Supportive	30
Use Age-Appropriate Resources	34
Foster Open Communication for Kids	39
Empowerment	43
Implementing Financial Literacy Activities	47
Conclusion	52
Epilogue	54
Afterword	55

Introduction

In today's increasingly complex and interconnected world, the ability to manage money effectively is a critical skill for success. Yet, financial literacy is often overlooked in traditional education systems, leaving many young people ill-prepared to navigate the complexities of personal finance. As parents, caregivers, and educators, it is our responsibility to fill this gap by teaching kids about money from an early age.

Teaching kids about money is about more than just imparting financial knowledge; it's about instilling essential life skills that will empower them to make informed decisions, set financial goals, and build a secure future for themselves. By equipping children with a strong foundation in money management, we can set them on the path to financial independence and success.

Within the pages of this book, we embark on a comprehensive exploration of the paramount significance surrounding the education of children in matters pertaining to finance. Our journey traverses the intricate landscape of financial literacy, delving deep into the core principles of money management and offering a plethora of pragmatic strategies and invaluable resources aimed at instilling fiscal acumen in the young minds of today's generation.

At its essence, this tome is a testament to the pivotal role that early financial education plays in shaping the trajectory of a child's fiscal future. Drawing upon a rich tapestry of research findings, insights gleaned from esteemed experts in the field, and the invaluable lessons distilled from real-life experiences, we illuminate the multifaceted facets of financial literacy with clarity and purpose.

Central to our discourse is an elucidation of the fundamental concepts underpinning money management—a mosaic that encompasses the nuances of earning, saving, spending judiciously, and investing wisely. Through a meticulous dissection of these principles, we empower parents, caregivers, and educators alike with actionable strategies designed to foster a holistic understanding of financial stewardship in the young charges under their care.

Within these pages, readers will find not only a compendium of theoretical knowledge but also a treasure trove of practical advice, borne out of the collective wisdom garnered from those who have traversed the terrain of financial education. From cultivating healthy financial habits to navigating the intricacies of budgeting and investment, each chapter is replete with actionable tips, insightful anecdotes, and hands-on activities tailored to facilitate experiential learning and lasting comprehension.

Moreover, this book serves as a beacon of inspiration, illuminating the trans-formative potential that lies within the realm of financial literacy. By empowering children with the tools and knowledge to navigate the complexities of the modern financial landscape, we sow the seeds for a future generation of financially savvy individuals—individuals equipped not only to weather the vicissitudes of economic uncertainty but also to thrive in a world where financial acumen is synonymous

INTRODUCTION

with personal empowerment and freedom.

In essence, this book is a testament to the trans-formative power of education—a road map that charts the course towards a future where financial literacy is not merely a privilege but a fundamental right bestowed upon every child. Through our collective efforts and unwavering commitment to the cause, we pave the way for a future generation empowered to seize control of their financial destinies and chart a course towards a brighter, more prosperous tomorrow.

Setting Financial Goals for Kids

SETTING FINANCIAL GOALS FOR KIDS

Establishing financial objectives stands as a pivotal milestone in the quest for fiscal prosperity and autonomy. This chapter endeavors to dissect the significance of instilling the practice of financial goal-setting in the younger generation, elucidating the manifold advantages that accompany this habit and furnishing pragmatic advice to aid children in formulating and accomplishing their financial ambitions. This systematic approach to financial planning serves as a road map toward achieving specific monetary targets and as a fundamental skill set that, when nurtured from an early age, lays the groundwork for lifelong financial literacy and responsibility.

The essence of setting financial goals lies in imbuing individuals with a sense of direction and purpose in their financial undertakings. For children, this practice demystifies the concept of money management, transforming abstract values into tangible objectives, be it saving for a coveted toy, funding a future educational endeavor, or simply accumulating a modest sum for discretionary spending. This distinction of financial objectives serves as a catalyzing force, motivating young savers and spenders alike to engage with their finances in a more deliberate and informed manner.

Beyond the intrinsic value of goal realization, the process of setting and striving towards financial targets harbors a wealth of developmental benefits. It cultivates a suite of competencies and virtues, including but not limited to, discipline, patience, decision-making, and the gratification that stems from self-efficacy. Moreover, this practice fosters an environment conducive to experiential learning, wherein children are afforded the opportunity to confront and navigate the repercussions of their financial choices, thereby internalizing the principles of cause and effect as they pertain to fiscal matters.

To translate the abstract notion of financial goal-setting into actionable strategies for children, a multi-faceted approach is recommended. This begins with the establishment of clear, achievable objectives, articulated in a manner that resonates with their developmental stage and personal interests.

Following this, the delineation of a structured plan to attain these goals is crucial, encompassing steps such as allocating a portion of their allowance or earnings towards their target, monitoring progress, and adjusting strategies as necessary. Additionally, the importance of visual aids and reinforcement mechanisms, such as charts to track savings or celebratory milestones to acknowledge achievements, cannot be overstated in their ability to maintain engagement and motivation.

In summation, the practice of setting financial goals embodies a cornerstone of financial education for children, equipping them with the tools and mindset required to navigate their fiscal futures with confidence and acuity. Through a combination of theoretical understanding and practical application, this chapter aims to empower caregivers and educators to instill a robust financial foundation in the younger generation, thereby facilitating a trajectory toward financial success and independence that extends well into adulthood.

Why Setting Financial Goals is Important for Kids:

Financial goals provide kids with a sense of direction and purpose when it comes to managing their money. By setting clear objectives, kids can stay motivated and focused on their financial journey. Moreover, financial goals help kids develop important life skills such as budgeting, saving, and investing, which are essential for long-term financial well-being. Setting financial goals also teaches kids the value of planning and foresight. By thinking ahead and setting goals for their money, kids learn to prioritize their spending and make informed financial decisions.

This not only helps them achieve their immediate goals but also lays the foundation for future financial success. Furthermore, setting financial goals instills in kids a sense of responsibility and accountability. When kids set goals for their money, they take ownership of their financial decisions and become more mindful of their spending habits. This empowers them to make wise choices with their money and develop healthy financial habits that will serve them well throughout their lives.

Teaching responsibility:

Inculcating the practice of financial goal-setting in children from an early stage is instrumental in sowing the seeds of fiscal responsibility. This educational approach transcends mere money management, embedding within young minds a profound understanding of the value of resources and the importance of foresight in their allocation. By guiding children to envision and articulate their financial aspirations, whether they are short-term desires or long-term ambitions, we lay the foundation for a mindset characterized by proactive engagement with one's financial future. This methodological introduction to financial planning not only encourages children to assume command over their economic circumstances but also cultivates a sense of accountability and self-reliance that is pivotal to their development into financially literate adults.

The act of setting financial goals engages children in a process of reflection and decision-making, compelling them to distinguish between whims and genuine needs, thereby prioritizing their expenditures and savings in alignment with their values and aspirations. This exercise in prioritization is not trivial; it mirrors the complexities of adult financial management, albeit on a scale appropriate to their age and understanding. Through this, children learn to appreciate the significance of deferred gratification—a concept critical to achieving long-term objectives over immediate, often fleeting, desires.

Furthermore, introducing goal-setting in financial education fosters an environment where independence and accountability are not just encouraged but required. Children who practice setting and working towards their financial goals develop a sense of ownership over their successes and failures. This sense of ownership is crucial; it transforms abstract concepts into tangible outcomes, making the lessons learned in the process deeply personal and therefore more impact. As children navigate the challenges of saving towards a goal, they encounter real-world financial principles first-hand, such as budgeting, saving, and the opportunity cost of their decisions.

This pedagogical (a method and theory of teaching) strategy does more than just teach children how to save; it imbues them with a holistic understanding of financial stewardship, emphasizing that financial decisions have consequences and that planning, persistence, and discipline are key to overcoming obstacles and achieving desired outcomes. Moreover, it fosters resilience, as children learn to adjust their strategies and continue striving towards their goals in the face of setbacks.

In essence, introducing children to the concept of setting financial goals is a multifaceted educational endeavor that equips them with the skills and mindset necessary for financial autonomy. It transforms the abstract notion of money management into a concrete framework of actionable steps toward achieving specific objectives, thereby demystifying the complexities of financial decision-making. This early foundation not only prepares children for the financial challenges of adulthood but also instills in them a sense of responsibility, independence, and accountability that transcends monetary matters, influencing their approach to various facets of life.

Promoting Financial Awareness:

The act of establishing financial objectives compels children to embark on a reflective journey through their fiscal landscape, necessitating a thorough appraisal of their current monetary status juxtaposed against their aspirations and necessities. This evaluative procedure is instrumental in awakening a heightened state of financial consciousness among young minds, guiding them through the intricacies of distinguishing between the essential and the extraneous. Such discernment paves the way for an informed prioritization of goals, underscoring the critical role of judicious financial planning and the prudent allocation of resources. Through this methodical approach, children are ushered into the realm of fiscal prudence, fostering an enriched comprehension of monetary value and the pivotal function of budgeting in safeguarding and augmenting one's financial journey.

Setting goals requires children to understand and manage various aspects of their finances. This involves an honest assessment of available resources, an acknowledgment of limitations, and a visionary outlook toward future acquisitions or achievements. It is within this contemplative space that children learn to reconcile their immediate wants with their long-term needs, thereby cultivating a strategic mindset towards expenditure and savings. This exercise in financial introspection and planning is invaluable, as it instills a foundational understanding of the finite nature of monetary resources, compelling a thoughtful consideration of how best to utilize these resources to fulfill both present and future aspirations.

The practice of setting and striving towards financial goals engenders a profound appreciation for the concept of budgeting. As children navigate the challenges of allocating their funds to meet their set objectives, they are inherently learning the art of financial stewardship—balancing the scales between current expenditures and future savings. This hands-on engagement with budgeting illuminates the critical balance required to manage finances effectively, highlighting the necessity of foresight, restraint, and adaptability in financial planning. Through these experiences, children gain invaluable insights into the mechanics of financial management, learning firsthand the impact of their financial decisions on their ability to achieve their goals.

Encourages Planning and Organization:

The practice of delineating financial targets propels children into a forward-thinking mindset, coaxing them to anticipate forthcoming needs and desires and to meticulously strategize for their attainment. This process initiates with the articulation of distinct objectives that encapsulate their financial aspirations, whether they be immediate goals such as purchasing a new toy or long-term ambitions like saving for college. Following the establishment of these benchmarks, children are then guided through the creation of actionable plans—a systematic approach that involves breaking down the overarching goal into manageable, incremental steps. This plan not only charts the course from current financial status to goal realization but also necessitates a thoughtful organization of their monetary resources. Through this structured approach, children are not merely learning to save; they are mastering the art of financial planning and management, acquiring a suite of skills that are fundamental to navigating life's financial waters.

This educational journey into the realm of financial goal-setting and planning imparts upon young learners a multifaceted skill set. At its core, it fosters an adeptness in planning—encouraging children to look beyond the immediacy of the present and to envisage a trajectory that leads to their desired financial future. This facet of financial literacy is invaluable, as it instills a sense of direction and purpose in their financial endeavors, ensuring that each monetary decision is a stepping stone towards their overarching objectives.

Simultaneously, the process of devising and adhering to a financial plan cultivates essential organizational skills. Children learn to categorize their financial activities, segregate their savings towards different goals, and monitor their progress with diligence and precision. This organizational prowess extends beyond the realm of finance, permeating other areas of their lives and fostering a general propensity for methodical thought and action.

Through the iterative process of planning, executing, and revising their financial strategies, children develop resilience and flexibility that are critical to successful financial management. They learn that setbacks are not failures but opportunities for learning and adjustment, a perspective that equips them with the adaptability required to navigate the inevitable financial fluctuations they will encounter in adulthood.

Fostering Discipline and Delayed Gratification:

Working towards financial goals instills discipline and teaches children the value of delayed gratification. They learn to resist impulse spending and prioritize long-term rewards over instant gratification, laying the foundation for sound financial habits and decision-making.

Building Confidence and Self-Esteem:

Achieving financial goals boosts children's confidence and self-esteem. It demonstrates their ability to set objectives, make informed decisions, and follow through with their plans, empowering them to take control of their financial future and pursue their dreams with confidence.

Providing a Sense of Purpose and Motivation:

Setting financial goals gives children a sense of purpose and motivation. It provides them with clear objectives to work towards, fueling their determination and enthusiasm as they strive to achieve their desired outcomes.

Preparing for Adulthood:

By teaching children how to set and achieve financial goals, parents and caregivers prepare them for adulthood. They equip them with the knowledge, skills, and mindset necessary to navigate the complexities of the financial world independently, empowering them to make informed decisions and build a secure future for themselves.

Saving and investing for kids

Teaching children the concepts of saving and investing is like planting seeds for their future financial security and prosperity. By instilling these principles at a young age, parents and caregivers empower children to develop lifelong habits of financial responsibility and wealth-building. In this guide, we will explore the importance of saving and investing for kids, provide practical tips for getting started, and offer guidance on how to nurture a child's financial journey.

Financial Responsibility:

Teaching kids to save and invest instills a sense of financial responsibility from a young age. By learning to manage their money wisely, children develop habits that will serve them well throughout their lives.

Long-Term Wealth Building:

The dual practices of saving and investing serve as potent mechanisms through which children can cultivate wealth gradually but steadily over time. By embarking on these financial endeavors at a young age, children avail themselves of a formidable advantage: the power of compounding interest. This trans-formative force, when harnessed early, has the potential to amplify their savings and investments exponentially, imbuing them with a distinct advantage in the pursuit of long-term financial security and prosperity.

At its core, saving entails the prudent allocation of a portion of one's income or resources towards future goals or contingencies. By setting aside funds in savings accounts or other low-risk vehicles, children lay the groundwork for financial resilience, accumulating a safety net that can shield them from unexpected expenses or facilitate the realization of their aspirations. Yet, it is the integration of investing into this financial paradigm that bestows upon children the opportunity to transcend mere accumulation and to propel their wealth toward greater heights.

Financial Independence: Saving and investing empower kids to take control of their financial future. By learning how to grow their money through saving and investing, children gain a sense of independence and self-reliance that will serve them well as they grow older.

Goal Achievement:

Saving and investing teach kids the importance of setting and achieving financial goals. Whether it's saving for a new toy, a college education, or their first car, children learn the value of setting objectives and working toward them diligently.

Risk Management:

Investing exposes kids to the concept of risk and reward. By learning how to assess risks and make informed investment decisions, children develop valuable skills that will help them navigate the financial markets with confidence.

Practical Tips for Saving and Investing with Kids:

Now that we understand the importance of saving and investing for kids let's explore some practical tips for getting started:

Set Savings Goals:

Help your child set specific savings goals that are meaningful to them.

Whether it's saving for a toy, a trip, or a future expense, having clear objectives will motivate your child to save diligently.

Encourage Regular Saving:

Encourage your child to save a portion of their allowance or earnings regularly. Set up a savings jar or piggy bank where they can deposit their money and make it a habit to save a certain percentage of their income each week or month.

Introduce the Concept of Investing:

As your child gets older, introduce them to the concept of investing. Teach them about different investment options, such as stocks, bonds, and mutual funds, and explain how investing can help grow their money over time. Begin by investing small amounts of money to help your child understand the basics of investing. Consider opening a custodial brokerage account or purchasing shares of a stock or index fund together as a learning experience.

Educate Through Experience:

Use real-life examples and experiences to teach your child about saving and investing. Take them to the bank to open a savings account, involve them in household budgeting discussions, and show them how their savings and investments grow over time.

Lead by Example:

Be a positive role model for your child by practicing good financial habits yourself. Show them how you save and invest your money and involve them in household financial decisions to help them understand the importance of responsible money management.

Celebrate Milestones:

Celebrate your child's savings and investment milestones to reinforce their progress and motivate them to continue working towards their financial goals. Whether it's reaching a savings target or earning their first dividend payment, acknowledge their achievements and encourage them to keep saving and investing.

Saving and investing are essential skills that lay the foundation for a child's financial future. By teaching children the importance of saving and investing from a young age and providing them with practical guidance and support, parents and caregivers empower children to take control of their financial destinies and build a secure and prosperous future for themselves. Through patience, education, and encouragement, we can help our children develop the skills and habits they need to thrive in an increasingly complex financial world.

Entrepreneurship Education for Kids

ENTREPRENEURSHIP EDUCATION FOR KIDS

Entrepreneurship education for kids is a specialized niche within the broader field of education that focuses on teaching children the principles of entrepreneurship, business management, and innovation. Here are some potential niches within entrepreneurship education for kids:

Young Entrepreneurs Workshops and Camps:

Workshops, camps, or boot camps are designed to introduce children to the world of entrepreneurship. This niche involves providing hands-on activities, group projects, and real-world simulations to teach kids about business concepts such as idea generation, product development, marketing, and sales.

Entrepreneurship Curriculum for Schools:

Comprehensive entrepreneurship curriculum for elementary, middle, and high schools. This niche involves creating lesson plans, activities, and resources aligned with educational standards to teach kids about entrepreneurship principles and skills.

Kidpreneur Clubs and Organizations:

Kidpreneur clubs or organizations within schools, community centers, or youth groups. This niche involves providing a supportive environment where children can learn, collaborate, and network with other aspiring young entrepreneurs, as well as access mentorship and guidance from adult entrepreneurs.

Online Entrepreneurship Courses for Kids:

Interactive online courses, tutorials, and webinars that teach children about entrepreneurship from the comfort of their homes. This niche involves developing engaging content, videos, and quizzes that cover topics such as business planning, financial management, and problem-solving skills.

Social Entrepreneurship Programs:

Programs and initiatives that teach kids about social entrepreneurship and how to use business principles to address social or environmental issues. This involves promoting values such as empathy, compassion, and social responsibility while empowering children to make a positive impact in their communities through innovative business solutions.

Entrepreneurship Resources for Homeschooling Families:

Curriculum guides, lesson plans, and educational materials tailored to homeschooling families interested in teaching their children about entrepreneurship. This niche involves offering flexible resources and activities that parents can use to incorporate entrepreneurship education into their homeschooling curriculum.

Entrepreneurship Coaching and Mentorship:

Offering one-on-one or group coaching services and mentorship programs for aspiring kidpreneurs. This niche involves providing personalized guidance, support, and encouragement to help children develop their entrepreneurial skills, overcome challenges, and achieve their business goals.

Make Learning Fun

In the fast-paced world of education, the quest to engage children in learning has never been more critical. In the pursuit of academic excellence, the idea of making learning enjoyable has gained significant momentum that delves into innovative strategies for infusing joy and excitement into the learning process. Let's explore some of the key insights and techniques from this book that aim to revolutionize education by making learning fun for kids.

The Magic of Play-Based Learning:

This emphasizes the trans-formative power of play-based learning in capturing children's attention and fostering a love of learning. By integrating play into educational activities, children can explore, experiment, and engage with concepts in a hands-on and meaningful way. Whether it's through imaginative play, outdoor exploration, or structured games and activities, play-based learning stimulates creativity, curiosity, and critical thinking skills. "Spark Joy" advocates for educators and parents to embrace play as a fundamental aspect of children's education, recognizing its ability to ignite a lifelong passion for learning.

Unleashing Creativity Through Arts Integration:

Arts integration offers a dynamic approach to learning that taps into children's creativity and imagination. This encourages educators to incorporate visual arts, music, drama, and dance into the curriculum to enrich children's learning experiences. By engaging in creative expression, children can explore concepts from multiple perspectives, make connections across disciplines, and unleash their innate artistic talents. Through arts integration, "Spark Joy" advocates for a holistic approach to education that nurtures children's creativity, self-expression, and appreciation for the arts.

Game Base Motivation Education for Engaging Learning Experiences:

This explores the concept of gamification as a powerful tool for creating engaging learning experiences. By incorporating elements of game design, such as challenges, rewards, and competition, educators can transform traditional lessons into interactive and immersive games. Gamification motivates children to actively participate in their learning, overcome obstacles, and achieve their goals. Whether it's through digital games, board games, or classroom activities, this advocates for the use of gamification to make learning enjoyable, memorable, and meaningful for children.

Storytelling as a Gateway to Learning Adventures:

Storytelling captivates children's imaginations and transports them to new worlds of learning adventures. highlighting the importance of storytelling in developing children's literacy skills, empathy, and cultural awareness. Through storytelling, children are exposed to diverse characters, cultures, and perspectives, fostering empathy and understanding of the world around them. By integrating storytelling into the curriculum, educators can inspire a love of reading, language, and learning that extends beyond the classroom. "Spark Joy" encourages educators to harness the power of storytelling to ignite children's curiosity, creativity, and passion for learning.

Exploring STEAM Education Through Hands-On Exploration:

Advocating for STEAM education (Science, Technology, Engineering,

Arts, and Mathematics) as a multidisciplinary approach to learning that fosters creativity, innovation, and problem-solving skills. By engaging in hands-on exploration and experimentation, children can apply concepts from science, technology, engineering, arts, and mathematics to real-world challenges and projects. "Spark Joy" emphasizes the importance of hands-on learning experiences in STEAM education, providing children with opportunities to explore, create, and innovate in a collaborative and supportive environment. Through STEAM education, "Spark Joy" aims to inspire children to become lifelong learners and innovators who are equipped to succeed in the 21st-century workforce.

Addressing Challenges and Pitfalls for Kids

MONEY AND FINANCE STRATEGIES FOR KIDS

Teaching kids about money management and objective setting is an invaluable investment in their future. However, along the journey to financial literacy, children may encounter various challenges and pitfalls that can hinder their progress. In this guide, we will explore common challenges faced by kids when learning about money and goal setting and provide practical strategies for addressing these obstacles effectively.

Peer Pressure and Materialism:

One of the most significant challenges kids may face is peer pressure and the influence of materialism. In a world where consumerism is prevalent, children may feel pressured to conform to their peers' spending habits and desires for material possessions.

Strategy:

Encourage kids to develop a strong sense of self-awareness and individuality. Teach them to differentiate between needs and wants and help them understand that true happiness does not come from material possessions. Encourage open communication about peer pressure and guide how to resist it confidently.

Addressing Challenges and Pitfalls for Kids:

Teaching kids about money management and goal setting is an invaluable investment in their future. However, along the journey to financial literacy, children may encounter various challenges and pitfalls that can hinder their progress. In this guide, we will explore common challenges faced by kids when learning about money and goal setting, and provide practical strategies for addressing these obstacles effectively.

ADDRESSING CHALLENGES AND PITFALLS FOR KIDS

Peer Pressure and Materialism:

One of the most significant challenges kids may face is peer pressure and the influence of materialism. In a world where consumerism is prevalent, children may feel pressured to conform to their peers' spending habits and desires for material possessions.

Strategy:

Encourage kids to develop a strong sense of self-awareness and individuality. Teach them to differentiate between needs and wants, and help them understand that true happiness does not come from material possessions. Encourage open communication about peer pressure and guide how to resist it confidently.

Impulse Spending:

Another common challenge for kids is impulse spending. With the prevalence of advertising and easy access to online shopping, children may be tempted to spend their money impulsively on items they don't really need or value.

Strategy:

Teach kids the importance of making thoughtful spending decisions. Encourage them to pause and consider their purchases before buying, asking questions like, "Do I need this?" and "Will this purchase bring me long-term satisfaction?" Introduce the concept of delayed gratification and help them set goals that require saving and planning.

Lack of Financial Education:

Many children may face challenges due to a lack of formal financial education. Without proper guidance and instruction, kids may struggle to understand basic money concepts and develop essential financial literacy skills.

Strategy:

Take an active role in your child's financial education by providing practical lessons and resources. Incorporate money management and goal-setting discussions into everyday activities, such as grocery shopping, budgeting for family outings, or saving for special occasions. Utilize age-appropriate books, games, and online resources to supplement their learning and make financial education engaging and enjoyable.

Fear of Failure:

Fear of failure can prevent kids from setting ambitious goals and taking risks. Children may be hesitant to set financial goals or make investment decisions for fear of making mistakes or falling short of their expectations.

Strategy:

Foster a growth mindset in your child by re-framing failure as a natural part of the learning process. Emphasize the importance of resilience and perseverance and encourage kids to view setbacks as opportunities for growth and learning. Celebrate their efforts and progress, regardless of the outcome, and provide support and encouragement to help them overcome their fears and take calculated risks.

Lack of Patience and Persistence:

ADDRESSING CHALLENGES AND PITFALLS FOR KIDS

Developing patience and persistence is essential for achieving financial goals, but it can be challenging for kids who are accustomed to instant gratification in today's fast-paced world.

Strategy:

Teach kids the value of patience and persistence by setting realistic expectations and breaking goals down into smaller, achievable milestones. Encourage them to celebrate their progress along the way and remind them that achieving significant goals takes time and effort. Model patience and persistence in your behavior and provide encouragement and support to help kids stay motivated and focused on their goals.

Be Patient and Supportive

BE PATIENT AND SUPPORTIVE

Parenting is a journey filled with challenges, triumphs, and endless growth opportunities. Amid the chaos and busyness of daily life, it's easy to lose sight of the importance of patience and support in nurturing our children, which explores the transformative power of patience and support in parenting.

Learning about money is a gradual process, so be patient and supportive as children navigate their financial education journey. Offer guidance and encouragement along the way and be willing to answer questions and provide explanations as needed.

Celebrate children's successes and milestones, no matter how small, and use setbacks as opportunities for learning and growth. Let's delve into some of the key insights and strategies from this book that highlight the profound impact of patience and supportiveness on children's well-being and development.

Cultivating Calmness Amid Chaos:

Parenting can be overwhelming at times, with demands coming from all directions and emotions running high. Emphasizing the importance of cultivating calmness and patience as a foundation for effective parenting. By taking a deep breath, pausing before reacting, and practicing mindfulness, parents can create a peaceful and supportive environment for their children to thrive. Rather than succumbing to frustration or impatience, encouraging parents to model patience and self-control, teaching children valuable coping skills and emotional regulation techniques.

Building Trust Through Unconditional Support:

Trust is a cornerstone of the parent-child relationship, and it is built on a foundation of unconditional support and acceptance. This advocates for parents to be a consistent source of love, encouragement, and understanding for their children, regardless of their successes or failures. By providing a safe and supportive space where children feel valued and respected, parents foster a sense of trust and security that enables children to explore, take risks, and learn from their experiences. Through unconditional support, empowering parents to nurture their children's self-esteem, resilience, and sense of belonging.

Empowering Through Positive Reinforcement:

Positive reinforcement is a powerful tool for encouraging desirable behavior and promoting positive self-esteem in children. Emphasizing the importance of recognizing and celebrating children's efforts, achievements, and progress, no matter how small. By offering specific praise, encouragement, and rewards for their accomplishments, parents reinforce positive behavior and motivate children to continue striving for excellence. Positive reinforcement builds children's confidence, self-esteem, and intrinsic motivation, fostering a growth mindset and a lifelong love of learning.

Embracing Mistakes as Opportunities for Growth:

Mistakes are an inevitable part of the learning process, and they offer valuable opportunities for growth and learning. This motivates parents to embrace mistakes as teachable moments and opportunities for children to develop resilience, problem-solving skills, and a growth mindset. Rather than focusing on perfection or avoiding failure, parents can support their children by offering constructive feedback, encouragement, and guidance as they navigate challenges and setbacks.

By re-framing mistakes as opportunities for growth and learning, empowering parents to cultivate resilience and perseverance in their children, and preparing them to overcome obstacles and thrive in an ever-changing world.

Fostering Independence Through Guided Support:

Independence is a crucial skill for children to develop, and it is nurtured through a balance of freedom and support from parents.

Advocating for parents to provide guided support that encourages children to take initiative, make decisions, and solve problems on their own. By offering guidance, encouragement, and resources, parents empower children to develop critical thinking skills, self-confidence, and a sense of autonomy.

Through guided support, enabling parents to nurture their children's independence while providing a safety net of support and guidance along the way.

Use Age-Appropriate Resources

USE AGE-APPROPRIATE RESOURCES

Age-appropriate resources play a crucial role in teaching kids about money. These resources should be engaging, easy to understand, and tailored to children's developmental stages. Here are some examples of age-appropriate resources for teaching kids about money:

For Preschoolers (Ages 3-5):

Picture Books: Colorful picture books with simple stories about money can help preschoolers grasp basic concepts such as counting coins, identifying different types of currency, and understanding the value of money. Look for titles like "The Bernstein Bears Trouble with Money" by Stan and Jan Bernstein or "Bunny Money" by Rosemary Wells.

Toy Cash Register: A toy cash register with play money can provide preschoolers with hands-on experience counting and sorting coins, making change, and engaging in pretend play scenarios such as shopping or running a store.

Money Flashcards: Flashcards featuring images of coins and bills along with their corresponding values can help preschoolers learn to recognize different types of currency and understand their worth.

Online Games and Apps: There are many educational games and apps designed specifically for preschoolers that teach basic math skills, including counting, sorting, and recognizing patterns. Look for apps like "Sesame Street: Elmo Loves 123s" or "PBS Kids: Ready to Learn.

Piggy Bank: A simple piggy bank can be a fun and interactive way for preschoolers to start learning about saving money. Encourage them to deposit coins or small bills into their piggy bank regularly and talk to them about the importance of saving for future goals.

6.2 For Elementary Schoolers (Ages 6-12):

Board Games: Board games like "Monopoly Junior," "The Game of Life Junior," or "Money Bags Coin Value Game" offer hands-on learning opportunities for elementary schoolers to practice counting money, making financial decisions, and understanding basic economic concepts.

Books and Workbooks: Look for age-appropriate books and workbooks that cover topics such as budgeting, saving, spending wisely, and entrepreneurship. Titles like "The Everything Kids' Money Book" by Brett McWhorter Sember or "The Kids' Money.

Allowance and Budgeting Tools: Introduce elementary schoolers to the concept of allowance and help them set up a simple budget to manage their money. Consider using tools like clear jars or envelopes labeled with different spending categories to help kids allocate their allowance toward saving, spending, and giving.

Online Resources: Websites and online platforms geared towards kids, such as "Practical Money Skills for Life" by Visa or "Money Confident Kids" by T. Rowe Price, offer interactive games, videos, and articles that teach financial literacy skills in a fun and engaging way.

Educational Videos: Platforms like YouTube offer a wealth of educational videos on topics ranging from basic money management skills to more advanced financial concepts. Channels like "Sesame Street," "Crash Course Kids," or "Khan Academy" feature videos that break down

USE AGE-APPROPRIATE RESOURCES

complex financial topics into kid-friendly lessons.

For Middle and High Schoolers (Ages 13-18):

Books and Magazines: Books and magazines geared towards teens can provide valuable insights into more complex financial topics such as budgeting, investing, managing credit, and preparing for college. Titles like "Get a Financial Life: Personal Finance in Your Twenties and Thirties" by Beth Kob Liner or "Teen Vogue's Guide to Money" offer practical advice and tips for teens.

Online Courses: Platforms like Coursers, Khan Academy or Junior Achievement offers a variety of online courses and resources focused on financial literacy for kids. The courses are interactive and designed to engage kids through real-world examples and activities offer online courses specifically designed to teach teens about personal finance. These courses cover a range of topics, from basic money management skills to advanced investment strategies, and can be completed at the student's own pace.

Financial Literacy Games: Interactive online games and simulations, such as "Financial Football" by Visa or "Stock Market Game" by SIFMA Foundation, allows teens to practice real-world financial scenarios in a risk-free environment and learn valuable money management skills.

Internships and Job Shadowing: Encourage teens to gain real-world experience with money by participating in internships or job shadowing opportunities in fields related to finance, business, or entrepreneurship. Hands-on experience can provide valuable insights and help teens develop practical skills for managing money in the future. By providing age-appropriate resources and opportunities for hands-on learning, parents, educators, and caregivers can empower children of all ages to become financially literate and responsible individuals who are equipped to navigate the complexities of the modern financial world.

Banking and Budgeting Apps: Introduce Teens to banking and budgeting apps that allow them to track their spending, set savings goals, and manage their money more effectively. Apps like Mint, YNAB (You Need a Budget), or Pocket Guard offer user-friendly interfaces and features tailored to teens' needs.

Foster Open Communication for Kids

from this picture you will understand that there is a super communication between the child and the father.

MONEY AND FINANCE STRATEGIES FOR KIDS

Money is a topic that can evoke strong emotions and complex dynamics within families. However, fostering open communication about money with kids is essential for their financial literacy and overall well-being. the importance of open communication and provides practical strategies for discussing money with children.

By following these strategies and incorporating financial education into everyday life, you can empower children to become financially responsible adults who are equipped to navigate the complexities of the modern financial world.

Remember that teaching kids about money is a journey, and the lessons you impart today will lay the groundwork for their financial success tomorrow.

Let's delve into some key insights and techniques from this book that can help parents and caregivers navigate conversations about money with their kids positively and constructively.

Creating a Safe and Non-Judgmental Environment:

The foundation of open communication about money begins with creating a safe and non-judgmental environment where children feel comfortable discussing financial topics. This emphasizes the importance of setting a tone of openness, trust, and respect in family conversations about money. By encouraging children to ask questions, express their thoughts and feelings, and share their perspectives on money matters, parents can foster a sense of security and openness that facilitates meaningful dialogue.

Age-Appropriate Conversations About Money:

This recognizes that conversations about money should be tailored to children's developmental stages and understanding. For younger children, discussions may focus on basic concepts such as the value of money, the importance of saving, and the difference between needs and wants.

As children grow older, conversations can become more complex, covering topics such as budgeting, earning, spending, and investing. By adapting the conversation to children's age and maturity level, parents can ensure that the information is relevant, relatable, and meaningful to their children's lives.

Leading by Example:

Parents are powerful role models when it comes to money management, and their behavior and attitudes toward money have a significant impact on children's financial habits and beliefs. importance of leading by example and demonstrating healthy financial behaviors such as budgeting, saving, spending wisely, and giving back to others.

By modeling responsible money management practices, parents can instill positive values and attitudes towards money in their children and provide them with a solid foundation for making informed financial decisions in the future.

Encouraging Curiosity and Questions:

Curiosity is a natural inclination in children, and parents can encourage this curiosity by inviting questions and fostering a spirit of inquiry about money-related topics. This encourages parents to be open and responsive to children's questions about money, providing accurate information and explanations in a way that is accessible and understandable.

By encouraging children to ask questions and seek answers, parents can empower them to develop critical thinking skills and financial literacy competencies that will serve them well throughout their lives.

Empowerment

this is the father advising and equipping the child about money management

Empowering kids about money is about more than just teaching them how to save or budget, it's about instilling in them a sense of confidence and competence to navigate the complex world of finance. We will delve into strategies for empowering children to take control of their financial futures.

Let's explore some key insights and techniques from this book that can help parents and educators foster financial empowerment in kids.

10.1 Encouraging Entrepreneurial Spirit:

Empowering Kids recognizes the value of fostering an entrepreneurial spirit in children as a means of empowerment. Whether it's starting a lemonade stand, launching a small business, or pursuing creative endeavors, entrepreneurship provides kids with opportunities to develop valuable skills such as creativity, problem-solving, and financial literacy.

By encouraging kids to explore their passions and pursue entrepreneurial ventures, parents and educators can instill in them a sense of confidence and self-reliance that will serve them well in all aspects of their lives.

Embracing Financial Independence:

This encourages parents and educators to support children in their journey toward financial independence. This means giving kids the freedom to make their own financial decisions, take calculated risks, and learn from their mistakes.

By allowing kids to experience the consequences of their actions in a safe and supportive environment, parents and educators can help them develop resilience, resourcefulness, and a sense of agency over their financial futures.

Cultivating a Growth Mindset:

Promoting the importance of cultivating a growth mindset in children regarding money. Rather than viewing financial challenges or setbacks as failures, kids are encouraged to see them as opportunities for growth and learning.

By fostering a positive attitude towards money and encouraging kids to persevere in the face of obstacles, parents and educators can empower them to overcome challenges and achieve their financial goals.

It's about instilling in them a sense of confidence, competence, and agency over their financial futures. By providing them with a solid foundation of financial knowledge and skills, encouraging entrepreneurial spirit, embracing financial independence, and cultivating a growth mindset, parents and educators can empower kids to take control of their financial destinies and build a secure and prosperous future for themselves young people ill-prepared to navigate the complexities of personal finance.

As parents, caregivers, and educators, it is our responsibility to fill this gap by teaching kids about money from an early age.

Teaching kids about money is about more than just imparting financial knowledge; it's about instilling essential life skills that will empower them to make informed decisions, set financial goals, and build a secure future for themselves. By equipping children with a strong foundation in money management, we can set them on the path to financial independence and success. In this book, we will explore the importance of teaching kids about money and provide practical strategies and resources for instilling financial literacy from a young age. Drawing upon research, expert advice, and real-life experiences, we will delve into the key concepts of money management and offer actionable tips for parents, caregivers, and educators alike.

Implementing Financial Literacy Activities

MONEY AND FINANCE STRATEGIES FOR KIDS

Kids should understand that money is earned by working. You can illustrate this by creating a simple chart or graph.

For example, draw a bar graph showing different chores (like cleaning up toys, making their bed, or helping with dishes) and assign a small amount of money they can earn for each task completed.

Inculcating the principles of monetary management in the minds of young learners encompasses a spectrum of pivotal teachings: the methodologies of accruing wealth, judiciously conserving it, the art of astute expenditure, and the strategic allocation of resources for investment purposes.

These foundational insights bestowed upon a kid, Is a toolkit of financial literacy, empowering them to navigate the fiscal landscapes of their futures with acumen and perspicacity. To distill these abstract concepts into tangible learning experiences, we shall delineate them through a series of simplified, yet captivating, pedagogical approaches, accompanied by illustrative graphical representations to crystallize each notion.

Introduce the concept of earning money through various avenues such as allowances for household chores, entrepreneurial ventures like a lemonade stand, or gifts.

The focus is on understanding that money is a reward for providing value or solving a problem.

Delving into the quintessential practice of amassing financial reserves, the act of saving money emerges as a cornerstone for ensuring economic stability and flexibility in the face of future necessities, unforeseen fiscal exigencies, and the aspiration towards significant acquisitions. This principle advocates for the meticulous allocation of a portion of one's income or resources, setting it aside in a disciplined manner, thereby creating a financial buffer that safeguards against the unpredictability of life's financial demands and the erosive effects of inflation over time.

The doctrine of saving is further enriched by the introduction of the concept of interest accumulation, a fundamental aspect of savings accounts and other similar financial instruments. Herein lies the compelling allure of compounding interest, a phenomenon where the interest earned on the principal amount is reinvested to generate additional interest, engendering a cycle of growth that exponentially increases the value of the initial savings. This mechanism serves as a powerful incentive, highlighting the trans -formative potential of letting one's money burgeon over periods of time through the strategic utilization of savings vehicles offered by financial institutions.

The strategic layering of this concept with the foundational practice of saving elucidates a multifaceted approach to financial prudence. It not only underscores the immediate utility of having readily available funds for emergent needs and desired expenditures but also showcases the long-term benefits of engaging with financial products designed to augment one's financial resources through the accrual of interest. In essence, the practice of saving, complemented by the savvy navigation of interest-bearing accounts, embodies a proactive engagement with one's financial future, advocating for a balance between present satisfaction and the anticipation of future prosperity.

In summation, the importance of saving money extends beyond the mere act of setting aside funds; it encompasses a broader strategy aimed at financial empowerment through the accumulation of wealth over time. By embracing the dual principles of saving and interest accumulation, individuals are equipped to navigate both the vicissitudes of immediate financial challenges and the pursuit of long-term financial goals, thereby instilling a robust foundation for economic resilience and autonomy.

Conclusion

As we draw the curtains on this odyssey through the realms of financial literacy, we are imbued with a profound sense of purpose and optimism. For within the pages of this book lie not merely words on paper, but a manifesto a rallying cry for the empowerment of future generations through the trans-formative power of financial education.

Throughout our exploration, we have traversed the labyrinthine corridors of money management, peeling back the layers of complexity to reveal the core principles that underpin fiscal acumen. We have delved deep into the recesses of research, drawn upon the wisdom of esteemed experts, and woven a tapestry of real-life experiences into the fabric of our discourse. In doing so, we have illuminated the path towards financial literacy—a path illuminated by the light of knowledge and paved with the stones of practical wisdom.

But our journey does not end here. No, it is merely the beginning—a prologue to a future where financial literacy is not a luxury reserved for the privileged few, but a birthright bestowed upon every child. For in our hands lies the power to shape the destiny of generations yet unborn—to instill within them the tools and knowledge necessary to navigate the complexities of the modern financial landscape with

CONCLUSION

confidence and aplomb.

As we turn our gaze towards the horizon, we are filled with a sense of urgency—a call to action that reverberates with the echoes of possibility. For the task that lies before us is great, but so too is the potential for change. Armed with the insights gleaned from these pages, we stand poised on the cusp of a new era—one defined not by financial insecurity and uncertainty, but by empowerment and opportunity.

So let us march forth, hand in hand, united in our commitment to the cause of financial literacy. Let us seize the reins of destiny and chart a course towards a future where every child has the opportunity to realize their full potential—a future where financial independence is not a distant dream, but a tangible reality.

In closing, let us remember that the journey towards financial literacy is not a solitary one, but a collective endeavor—one that requires the concerted efforts of parents, caregivers, educators, and policymakers alike. Together, we can build a world where financial literacy is not just a goal, but a fundamental cornerstone of a brighter, more prosperous tomorrow.

Epilogue

Afterword

Following their participation in the financial literacy program, children enthusiastically adopted prudent saving habits, allocating portions of their allowances towards future aspirations. Their piggy banks brimmed with coins, symbolizing their commitment to fiscal responsibility. Engagement in investment clubs ignited a fascination with stocks, fostering a deeper understanding of financial markets. Through immersive budgeting exercises, they discerned between desires and essentials, equipping them with invaluable money management skills. Empowered by newfound knowledge, they embarked on a lifelong quest for financial security, poised to navigate the complexities of personal finance with confidence and foresight.

www.ingramcontent.com/pod-product-compliance
Lightning Source LLC
Chambersburg PA
CBHW070417230526
45471CB00006B/2843